COOKING UP SUCCESS

Helping You Discover the Job of Your Dreams

CINDY ETSELL

Cooking Up Success

Second edition published in 2016 by

Panoma Press Ltd
48 St Vincent Drive, St Albans, Herts, AL1 5SJ, UK
info@panomapress.com
www.panomapress.com

Book design and layout by Neil Coe.

Printed on acid-free paper from managed forests.

ISBN 978-1-784520-92-2

Dedication

For my mother who taught me never to give up, for friends and family, and especially William who is my rock, my best friend and with me every step of the way.

Contents

Introduction

Do you find yourself stuck in a job you dislike? Are you facing redundancy, nearing retirement or just feel ready to make some changes to find the job you love? Are you finding it tough to know how to take that first step?

There are lots of books on the market and I wanted to create something different using a metaphor that we relate to every day regardless of who we are, where we live and what makes us tick. It was important for me to make the journey enjoyable and dare I say fun, hence 'cooking up success'. We take your raw materials and together cook up a recipe for your success!

Working through this book you will learn how to:

- Figure out your core skills and values and how to turn those elements into creating and finding the job you desire

- Create your personal 'toolkit' for change

- Develop and nurture your 'network' – these are the people who support, recommend and offer you guidance and help when you need it most

- Create your recipe or picture of your desired state and new role

- Pull everything together and write the CV that will change your job and life

- Look at the role of goal setting, with guidance on acting on those goals throughout your life

- Prepare yourself for interviews and negotiation

- Achieve success in finding that role and what comes next – longer term career planning

I wrote this book based on my personal experiences to help you find your way through the maze that is the job hunt. Food is used throughout the book as a metaphor for change. I wanted to help others avoid some of the minefields I encountered.

What makes this book different and how does it work?

It is written in two parts:

Part A

The cooking process – steps used based on a simple pasta recipe; complex or simple, the process remains the same.

This demonstrates the connection between having the right ingredients to create a meal and hopefully shows you what skills you have today and what you might need to create your perfect job.

Part B

Using the same 'steps found in a recipe' we show you how to apply this to making a career change from a very basic starting point to the complete 'dish' – your new role or career.

We take your raw ingredients and together cook up a recipe for your success!

Included are food bytes, examples, exercises and suggestions from Cindy's recipe box along with suggested readings to bring the concept alive. These are tools that helped me initially and continue to drive my career path. These are personal stories and examples which I used over the past 20 years in my career and job search. So come and join me in one of my workshops and put it to the test.

My mission is to show you how to change your life, identify what makes you happy and ultimately get the job you want! For demonstration purposes, I have used a simple recipe as an example. The recipe is a guide only; it allows you to begin your journey slowly and makes a great starting point to making a change in your career.

Setting the Scene

So Why Food and Career Change?

Food is something everyone can relate to, whether through cooking, dining out, travelling or watching TV.

I believe magic happens when you talk about food, everyone can relate to it in one way or another. It is about taste, experimentation, and these days every possible ingredient is available.

When trying to figure out how to make the book work I took career development and search to a different level. I thought what would happen if we used 'ingredients' and applied the same concept to individuals?

A picture emerged of Cooking up Success. All of us have tried to create a meal out of nothing. We take a few simple ingredients, find a recipe or make one up and the outcome is a meal. There is no such thing as failure, just flavour. The same applies if we have too many ingredients – sometimes simplicity does the trick.

THAT IS HOW WE LEARN! To make the book fun, easy to use and follow I set it up in steps which are broken down into A and B. Hopefully by the time you have finished you will have developed your own personal career and are well on your way to finding the job you desire.

"Choose a job you love and you will never have to work a day in your life."

Confucius

Welcome to Cooking up Success – your guide to creating the career you desire!

Food creates the magic, it breaks downs barriers, all we need to do is open the door to our imaginations and explore. The same applies to making a career change. Finding what you love and identifying your core skill can be both exciting and daunting but worth the journey.

Are you ready to take that first step? Do you have the intention, desire and commitment to focus and make a change? All you need is patience, focus and an open mind to making your dream a reality.

Do any of these statements sound familiar? If you can relate to even one then this book is for you:

- I am over 40 and would love to make a change but who will hire me?

- I wish I could do something else that pays better and offers me flexibility

- How come everyone gets promoted and not me?

- My boss keeps giving me more to do and I don't know what more I can do, I am already maxed out

- I am so bored and want a new challenge but where do I start?

- I would love to do a job where I could give something back

- I want to spend more time with my children

- I don't have a work/life balance but that is the price I pay for a good salary

- What will happen if they pick me for redundancy?

- I feel invisible

- Networking events terrify me, why do we have to do this?

- I love travelling but I have too much work to take a holiday

When facing change within an organisation most people rarely prepare because they believe redundancy will not happen to them. Very few people start out working with a clear career path in mind.

Putting our heads in the sand will not save or protect us from change. Did you know that most of us spend more time planning a summer holiday than creating and committing to developing our career?

I was recently asked to do a presentation on 'What is wrong with career management?' My immediate response was what is career management? How many people plan ahead and how many fall into a role out of university with no idea why or how they got the job and what will happen down the road? If you are one of the few who plan ahead, well done. In my experience we are focused on getting a job when we finish school. The choices when we leave school are more about finding a job fast so we can start paying off student loans, finding somewhere to live and therefore the first role offered is the one accepted and our work journey begins. In a blink of an eye, we hit our mid-

30s then 40s and wonder where the time went and realise that we are not doing what we love, life is moving way too fast and our work/life balance is non-existent.

The question is what to do next with the skills and experience I have and who will recruit me if I am over 40? Many of the statements listed earlier run though our minds when the realisation hits that our career is broken, it needs to be fixed but how and where does one start?

Many larger employers offer personal development programmes, usually online, which are supposed to be covered in our appraisals but for many employers and employees it is merely a tick in the box. The ownership of our career is for each individual to own, create and ask for help in terms of mentoring, training and guidance from our colleagues, friends and our employers. It is vital that each employee takes responsibility for their personal growth. Every corporate organisation I worked for offered personal development plans but I know I rarely utilised it except around appraisal time. Even when I took the time to work through a plan my boss did not take it into account. So why go to all the hassle and expense and then not utilise it? The intention is there but then both the employer and employee don't have the time or inclination to do anything more than put a tick in the box. Only when I finally took responsibility for my advancement and change did I understand the importance of creating and following a career and life plan. Where are you? Do you know what is next for you?

One example that stands out for me was in November 1995 when the company I worked for in Canada offered me an incredible opportunity to move to the UK for an

EMEA role, working with others to set up our business successfully in Europe. As a senior salesperson it was a terrifying prospect but exciting. I thought I would move to the UK for two years, improve my skills and knowledge and spend time getting to learn and see all parts of Europe. Twenty years later and I still live in London.

As a successful salesperson I never worked in an office full-time, never commuted and had little knowledge of marketing but thought why not and the die was cast. Little did I know what awaited me: a company looking for a buyer and telling me that within one year I would not have a job and neither would members of the team!

My first taste of corporate life in the big city was unexpected and I felt let down and terrified. What was I going to do next?

I panicked, I had never not worked and my network in the UK was small. I contacted people through my network in North America and the UK and let them know I was on the job hunt. Luckily I had a severance package and a new job as a marketing director; I had to travel miles, drive and navigate and put up with challenges I never imagined. I was stressed, then ill and after nine months realised this company was not for me. I planned my exit and resigned with some notice and no other role. I was scared. I will come back to this later in the book but this experience was really the first part of my journey into the realisation and importance of forward planning. As I get older I realise that if I had planned ahead I never would have taken that role. I advise people to breathe and take the time to figure out their next steps before jumping at the first role offered.

I wrote a CV, knowing some of my skills, for example sales and marketing, which allowed me to pursue a dream but it would take more time to form a clear picture.

Before we move on I think it is important to set the scene in regards to the job market in the UK. I want to offer some background and insights which demonstrate the opportunities and changes happening in the UK and other markets which have a huge impact on every person regardless of age or career path.

The stats from May to July 2015 state that there are 31 million in work, with 22.74 million in full-time and 8.36 in part-time employment. What was also very interesting is that one in seven workers in the UK now work for themselves. The Office of National Statistics states that 4.54 million are self-employed which is up 8% from the same time a year ago. That is incredible and makes me wonder if this trend will continue.

The biggest rise is in the number of older workers: the over 50s up 36% from 10 years ago.

As baby boomers we thought we could have it all, we want to work but also enjoy balance and doing something we love. We were that generation whose mothers tended to stay at home, they did not have the same opportunities and when I was a child we were asked what we wanted to be when we grew up. My mother's generation with rare exceptions were never asked what they wanted to do with their life. It was assumed they would marry and have children. What struck me as incredible when I was home for my mother's funeral was my sister told me that when my mother married she had to quit her job. Today that sounds incredible but I guess then that was the norm versus the exception. She did go back to work because she had no choice but her dream was to be a nurse. When that was not realised she went for the next best choice and worked in the hospital as a ward clerk. She did that job for 40 years with a smile and passion, touching everyone in her path in a positive way.

As one of those over 50 I believe there is huge opportunity and in this ever changing market we must be prepared and understand what we have to offer the marketplace today and in the future. If we don't keep up with change it will be forced upon us and we will face change sooner than you think. Stepping out of your comfort zone will give you the courage to face your fear and grab the incredible opportunities waiting for you.

At the moment in the UK, according to the BBC, we have a huge skills gap in 43 main areas especially within engineering. According to the CBI nearly 40% of firms are looking for staff and have had difficulty finding the right person and 50% felt it would get worse. It seems millennials (born after 1977) who reached adulthood around 2000 want variety and tend to change jobs on average every 18 months. This will soon be the norm as technology enables us to work anywhere. I meet many who have worked in the same company for 10 to 20 years; this will be unheard of in the future.

The baby boomers (born after the war in 1946 to 1964) comprise a large portion of the current workforce. They were told they could have it all and have seen incredible change within the job market. I was fortunate being in sales where technology was used to make my life easier. I remember my first laptop, it weighed 15 pounds and used the DOS operating systems. Windows was welcomed with open arms – wow, it made life easier and it was assumed we had the knowledge and skills to use the technology.

In his book *Rebooting Work* Maynard Webb says until now companies not employees have been in charge. He believes that companies have called the shots where people work and when but the world of work is shifting. This is reinforced in the stats above where the UK has a huge shortfall of talent. Maynard states that studies show the supply of people able to understand and respond to business challenges will fall short of what is needed in the future. Once we identify our skills we can apply our skills and experience to a variety of different industries and achieve greater personal freedom. Having worked at Cisco for five years, they practised what they sold and allowed us to work in virtual teams from anywhere. The technology is there, but some companies still believe employees should work in an office for a set period every day which I believe will change drastically as people want more freedom and challenge.

In my role at Cisco I covered all Europe as a Retail and CPG specialist and got to work with some amazing people and companies learning every step of the way. I was on a plane pretty much every week and because of technology always connected. This is good and bad as it can create challenges around your work/life balance. If we don't set boundaries when we begin our career we lose sight of what is important and can become unhappy, ill and disillusioned. I finally realised this after a few years of having no life except work which I loved. I visited incredible cities and experienced great food, culture and was lucky to be intellectually challenged daily. My work day started most days at 7am when my phone went on and did not end until midnight. I would clear my in-box on Saturday and by Monday morning it was full yet again. Welcome to the virtual world where we are always on! It is up to us to set our boundaries before we start working for a specific company otherwise you will end up burnt out and in trouble. Have you set your boundaries?

According to a survey in *Personnel Today* on 1 September 2013, one in six UK employees are experiencing anxiety, stress and depression in the workplace. These statistics produced by mental health charity MIND indicate that the line between work and personal life has become increasingly blurred. Technological developments, combined with the constant stream of business, mean that being contactable 24/7 has become a necessity for the majority of UK workers. Information overload they say is part of everyday life so we must make a conscious decision to remove ourselves from this barrage.

I know only too well the impact this can have on our health and relationships so if you feel overwhelmed now is the time to act. Take control and make the necessary changes to get that balance back.

I was in London for a networking event which started at 6pm in the City. The Tube was packed. What struck me as I walked from Monument station was the steady stream of people spilling out like a river at exactly the same time, creating chaos on the streets and the Tube. Imagine a London where companies embraced mobile working or flexible working. I for one would love to see happier commuters and people with the opportunity to enjoy this incredible city.

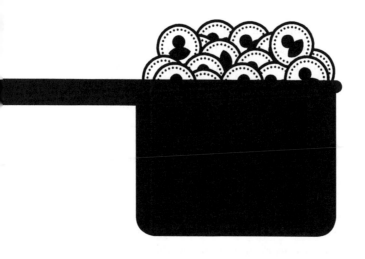

Part A Step 1:
Creating Something out of Nothing

"Creativity is not so much a boundless well, but an all-you-can-eat buffet of elements for your creative endeavour. Eventually you have eaten your fill, and it's time to digest and then make something."

Vera Nazarian - *The Perpetual Calendar of Inspiration*

Why do I open this book with food? When you walk in your house after work, after that horrible commute what is the first thing you do? Take off your coat, get comfortable, maybe pour a drink and think about what to eat? All of us are faced with this dilemma every single day; some people are much better at planning ahead so they have food prepared but in my experience they are in the minority. Others pick up takeaways or order in, some eat food like crisps or biscuits. What about you?

When you arrive home and open your cupboards and fridge, are you confronted with too many or not enough choices? When we work and commute this decision can sometimes overwhelm us so we end up with takeaways or food that will not give us the energy we need to make decisions or work that needs to be completed.

When you look at your choices of what to make, what do you find? Ingredients to make a simple meal, or are you overwhelmed by choice? I open the book this way because I want to draw the analogy to work and our life balance. If we forget to buy groceries for the week then we end up spending more money or not having the right food to eat. Being prepared makes life so much easier. What if we applied the same rules to sorting out our jobs, careers and goals? We spend a substantial part of our lives working so wouldn't it be nice to find a job we love that meets our core needs?

Cindy's Recipe Box - Larder

I have a store of basic ingredients so I can make something fast and nutritious. Pasta is a mainstay and I always have several types in my larder. These simple ingredients can be used in different ways but I chose a simple pasta dish.

My larder (core ingredients)

- eggs
- pasta
- courgette
- garlic
- parmesan cheese
- green onion
- can of chopped tomatoes
- frozen basil
- salt and pepper
- olive oil

Combining these ingredients what can I make? Something quick, tasty, nutritious that looks fabulous!

- An omelette, pasta or a frittata?

- My choice was pasta because of its versatility and nutritious value.

- You can add anything you like to change or adjust the taste and create an amazing plate of food.

- A store cupboard is a good idea, all you need is dried pasta, dried mushrooms, canned items such as tuna, salmon, anchovies and tomatoes as with these you can flavour with little effort.

- If you found too much choice in terms of ingredients you might choose to make something different. Some shoppers or foodies go mad and buy more food than they need. They are captured by packaging or brand. Sometimes having too much choice can make your decision on what to cook tough.

- For simplicity the recipe chosen is easy. Even if you are not an experienced cook this recipe is easy to follow. If you decide to make something other than the recipe I use, just follow the steps which can be found in almost every recipe.

Food byte:

If you change the ingredients you change the outcome. An example would be adding chilli or goat's cheese to the sauce. I have done both and the flavour is great, just taste as you go.
The same applies to your skills.

Part B Step 1:
Core Skills
(Laying the Foundation)

*"Attitude is a little thing that makes
a big difference."*

Winston Churchill

Just like ingredients, each of us through our experiences and personalities has our own personal map of the world. Are we unsure about what our recipe is, who we are and what makes us tick?

Having some key ingredients when making a meal is a great starting point. The same applies to our work and careers.

Understanding what makes us happy, sad, challenged, tired or excited, our background, history, education is part of our journey of knowing what makes us tick. Each of us is different, which is why working through exercises we come out knowing what we love to do, which makes our journey easier when it comes to acknowledging our core skills, our strengths and weaknesses – all essential elements for growth and success.

I come from a large family. My mother had to work so she relied on all of us to help when it came to cooking or doing what was necessary to run a home. I learned to cook at a young age and that meant cooking for large numbers, usually 8 to 10 people. I spent hours watching my mum and grandmother bake and was curious so I asked lots of questions and watched and learned. Money was scarce and with many mouths to feed my mother never wasted anything.

When I was eight I decided to make an apple pie. I thought it would be easy – after all, I had watched my grandma and mother make them often and so I thought how hard can it be? I got everything ready and was pleased as punch when the pastry worked. My grandmother's tip was when making pastry make sure you have cold hands and a cold pastry board and don't work the flour too hard. Sounds easy but it is much harder than it looks. To this day my pastry is a challenge.

I started to do the filling and realised we were short on apples. I did not know what to do so I asked my grandmother who suggested I look to see what other fruit was available.

We had blueberries which I used to mix with the apples. I was upset as I wanted my apple pie to be perfect like my grandma's, she always had the lightest touch when it came to pastry and especially pies.

She saw the tears, asked me what was wrong and smiled. She reached down and gave me the biggest hug and said, "This is your apple pie, made with love and I know it will taste great."

That started my love affair with food and learning what and how to substitute ingredients to create my own special version of pie. I used the same idea throughout my career, thinking what can I offer the marketplace from a skills perspective?

When working in freelance recruitment during the boom in 1999, everyone wanted the right people with the perfect skills for their freelance role. I found we didn't have candidates with a specific industry background but recognised they had the skills; for instance, if the position was for a direct marketing person within telecommunications. I called the decision maker and convinced him that skills were far more important than the industry knowledge which could be learned. They ended up recruiting a direct marketer from the publishing industry and were so impressed her contract kept getting extended.

Unfortunately, as many people have experienced, recruiters find it difficult to think outside the box and I cannot blame them as they try to fill a very specific brief from the client. Recently I have seen recruiters trying to do things differently.

Taking time to understand your skills, strengths and weaknesses will lay a strong foundation when it comes to writing your CV.

Just like ingredients needed to create your perfect dish you can use the same process to document your key skills. I work with people from 30 to 60 and find many do not know what they love to do in a typical workday. I am passionate about helping people discover the career they love especially those in the above age range where our goals and focus change drastically as we move further down our career and life path. Our priorities change and many realise they want to spend their time doing what makes them happy while trying to find a work/life balance.

We spend so much of our lives working yet many people are tired, frustrated, unhappy and looking for answers. As you work though this book we will take a step-by-step process of realising what makes us tick and why. As we move through that learning you will be able to create a CV that reflects who you are and why you stand out and should be recruited.

Grab a pen and paper, find a quiet space, think about your core skills or ingredients – name a few things you love to do that make you smile! Aim for at least 10 and don't be afraid to ask friends and colleagues to give you feedback. It is tough for us sometimes to see our key strengths.

Exercises from Cindy Recipe Box

Take a break, grab a pen and notebook. I suggest using the same notebook or you may prefer using a tablet or laptop. Don't think too hard, just write what comes into your mind until you have at least five skills listed.

Here a few examples of core skills:

Self-starter, organised, decisive, strong attention to detail, budgeting, love working with customers, completer / finisher, financial acumen etc.

If you found this exercise difficult, think about your current role and what your daily tasks consisted of, what you enjoyed and what you disliked.

Remember your last appraisal – what feedback did you receive? Feedback is tough to give and receive and it is human to feel defensive. My advice is to listen and try to keep an open mind. Be very honest with what is being said, always bearing in mind who is giving that advice and the manner in which it is delivered.

I was told once that I was not technical enough. I thought about it and made a point of getting stuck into a few courses but also realised that the skills I did have, the ability to show the value that technology brings to business to help solve problems, was more valuable given the role I was doing in business development. However I listened to the advice and acted accordingly.

> ## Food byte:
> *During my career I found some of the best feedback I got was from my colleagues and customers. I learned so much about how others saw me and was able to adjust my behaviour accordingly to get a positive outcome.*

Even with limited ingredients it is incredible what can be made out of very little. When you are ready repeat the earlier exercise and see if you can add a few more core skills. In the UK there is a shortage of specific skills. In the opening chapter I mentioned that many believe the skills shortage will worsen especially within engineering and technology. What that says is if this is one of your skills and background, finding a role is easier. Or if this is an area of interest then maybe there is an opportunity to take some courses and change your career path.

Technology changes rapidly, it is impossible for companies to keep up and fill the gaps in the market. As an individual, depending on your current or desired field, do a bit of research to see what is lacking in your specific area. For instance, working within the software industry I have seen a huge increase in demand for Java programmers and those with a background in analytics or 'big data' as it is called. What about your industry, where do you fit? It is vital you understand your industry's issues so you are informed when speaking to recruiters or future employers.

If you see a specific industry sector where you would like to work, there are great courses available to gain additional skills or level of expertise. Also volunteer work is a great asset for testing your skills and learning.

Food byte:

Skill is defined as the ability to do something well, or expertise, so go and find that skill and continue to fine-tune your expertise. Keep that CV up to date.

Part A Step 2:
Essential Cooking Tools

*"Accept yourself, your strengths,
your weaknesses, your truths and know
what tools you have to fulfil your purpose."*

Steve Maraboli – *Life, the Truth and Being Free*

So are you ready to start your cooking? What if you just realised you didn't have the right tools or equipment to make it work successfully? What would you do? Improvise, borrow the necessary equipment? There are numerous gadgets that take longer to use than the old-fashioned knife and chopping board. So if they ask for the latest chopper, a good knife does the trick; maybe your cooking might take more time but as long as you are prepared everything will work out well. The same practice applies to each of us as we search for our higher purpose – our next job or new business.

This step outlines some of the essential tools needed when following a recipe and making your ideal dish successfully. When I make pasta it would be really difficult to achieve my desired outcome without the big pot to boil the water in or the pasta. This seems quite simple but how many people have the right tools ready for their career?

- Measure the pasta: dried pasta about 1 cup per person, it doubles in volume when cooked

- Fill a saucepan with water, cover and put on high heat until it comes to a rolling boil

- Use a large frying pan, large enough to hold the pasta and sauce

- Get out your chopping board

- Sharp knife (handle with care)

- Spoon to stir the sauce

- Strainer to drain the pasta

- Grater for the cheese – if you don't have one you can use a potato peeler

- Teaspoon to taste the sauce as it cooks – make sure you taste at different stages so you know what to add

- Depending on what you plan to cook you might need a different set of tools

- There are lots of new gadgets on the market designed supposedly to make our lives easier! A word of caution: make sure you know how to use them as they can sometimes take ages to figure out

Food byte:

I decided it would be faster to use a mandolin to slice my vegetables but by the time it was set up I could have chopped them faster with a sharp knife. The same would apply to making changes in your life — there is so much noise out there that sometimes it is difficult to know what tools you need.

Part B Step 2:
Toolkit for Change

"It's not what happens to you that determines how far you will go in life, it is how you handle what happens to you."

Zig Ziglar

Remember some of these statements:

- If I leave this job even though I hate it who else will offer me another job?

- I wish I could so something I love but I have no idea where to start

- Life is not fair sometimes, how come my colleagues with less experience and expertise get promoted and not me?

- I wish I could earn more money so I could travel and help out my children

- I heard they may downsize in our department but I will wait and see what happens, I should be fine

- I have never had to look for a job so I don't have a CV as I have never had to do one, I would not know where to start

- I feel invisible because I am over 50, who will offer me another job?

The statements above are just a few examples of what I hear within the offices and when I coach those facing change within their work environment. Whether that change is redundancy, retirement, a new boss or change of department, it is difficult.

I was made redundant four times. The first was a major shock, I felt like someone had pulled the rug out from under me and I was frozen, not quite believing this could happen to me. I had moved my life and left everything behind for a new role and an adventure. Now what should I do?

I had two choices: do nothing and see what happened or take control of my life and make change happen. Luckily I was offered some outplacement which helped hugely because I took advantage of all the tools and consulting on offer. I worked hard, faced some truths and pushed myself to understand what was important to me in terms of values and then worked to create a career plan.

Therefore the next three times I was made redundant I found the change was easier because I had the tools to face the challenge but it was still really tough. I found it hard not to take it personally; although it is personal, it is a decision taken by the company which has more bearing on their strategy and focus than on individuals.

If some of the statements above resonate or you too are facing redundancy for the first or third time, remember you are not alone. The world is changing especially when it comes to work lives. Career planning is something we seldom think about until it is broken and change is forced upon us. Ask your friends if they have a career plan. Don't be surprised by their response. I see redundancy as a second chance, an opportunity to take the time and decide what you want to do with your life, not only in terms of career but life in general.

This step is filled with tips and examples of what helped me survive and grow after each redundancy. I hope it helps pave the way and smooth your path.

What are you going to cook with? How are you going to get the change you want to achieve your desire?

In this step we consider areas like attitude, networking and other tools that are essential in creating the meal or the life you want.

A great analogy is a chef who always has their own 'tools'; their knives stay with them through their career, they are precious and essential to their success. What tools do you believe are essential for your success?

Success is defined by you, not anyone else. Whatever we believe will happen! I know that sounds like a powerful statement. I remember buying my first car in the UK. I test drove quite a few and I was fortunate enough to have a car allowance. I thought what about a BMW? In Canada they cost a fortune so I started my research and ended up buying a used 3-series BMW in a teal colour. Before I made the purchase I did research and tried to talk to others who had owned something similar but it was nowhere to be found. Funny, after the purchase was complete everywhere I looked there it was, which I found very odd. Has that ever happened to you, whether it was the purchase of car, home, laptop?

Our brains are incredible, we have the reticular activating system (RAS), or extra thalamic control modulatory system, which is a set of connected nuclei in the brain of vertebrates that is responsible for regulating wakefulness and sleep-wake transitions. Basically in layman's terms this is a place where your thoughts, internal feelings and the outside influences converge. It is very skilled in producing dynamic effects on the motor activity centres located in the brain and the cortex activity such as the frontal lobes. That is why goal setting is very important. Our brain remembers.

If you think you are going to have a bad day, you will. If you believe everyone will be successful except you, then that will happen. The good news is by setting your goals and developing your toolkit to change, you draw the right things into your life and are more in control of the outcome. There is an appendix at the end of the book on goal setting but it is mentioned here because it is crucial to success. Another way to bring your desires and goals alive is through creative visualisation.

Examples from Cindy Recipe Box

Ever make a new big purchase like a new house or something simpler like a washing machine or vacuum cleaner? After the purchase did you see the same item everywhere? In the paper, an advert, heard about others buying the same item? Remember that expression, 'be careful what you wish for'; be clear on your thoughts as we have a way of drawing the good and the bad to us unless we are very aware.

This is the start of an exciting recipe gathering the components that help formulate your ingredients for life with your ever present toolkit. Are you ready?

We have our own map of the world which is a result of our experiences, good and bad, and those help us when we seek to establish a key set of ingredients. Throughout the many ups and downs in life, attitude is a key and necessary component, it makes all the difference.

How many people come with incredible educational background and skills but have challenges finding the right job? Or they get to the interview stage and are not successful.

Those who believe what happens to them is down to others and not them.

Working in a corporate environment my attitude literally saved me from many difficult and challenging situations. I worked with someone who was very capable but did not believe in their ability. Does this sound familiar? They made others around them uncomfortable, blaming them for bad outcomes which were their responsibility. Before meetings I took out my well-worn copy of *Attitude* and read it over.

We cannot change what this person does or says but we are in complete control of how we respond to any given situation. Change the way you respond and you will change the outcome. Trust me, it works every time!

We all have our own map of the world which is a result or culmination of how we were brought up, our experiences, good and bad. I think the most powerful example of this happened with my father. He was not an easy man, difficult to say the least, and he and I did not get along well. He would say something just to get a reaction from me, and I took the bait every time. Then I read an article about attitude. The next time he said something I didn't like, I was ready and I changed my reaction completely. I was calm and replied in a gentle voice. After that I never had a problem again. Powerful.

Another example is working for the London Training and Enterprise Council based in Hounslow. We ran an incredible programme delivered by The Pacific Institute called STEPS, which was run for the long-term unemployed, called New Deal. Part of the programme teaching was about how our brain works, remember the RAS mentioned earlier? A few of the clients came from a housing estate in the middle of England where high unemployment, crime and drugs were rampant. During the training you could almost see their light bulb moment when they realised they could change their behaviour, take control and make a difference. These few people managed to turn that housing estate around because they had a positive can-do attitude.

All of us face personal and professional challenges in our lifetime regardless of age, culture, or status. Many times we think we can control outcomes or life, which of course is a fruitless exercise.

My experience tells me we cannot control other people or situations but we can control how we react to those situations. How many times have we said if only I had a new car, great job, life partner then I would be happy? We may meet that person and then try and change them to what we think they should be; guess what, that does not work. Accept people for who they are and together help each other shine. Trying to control outcomes never works. As my mother used to say when she was teaching me to cook, read the recipe, follow your instinct but nothing ever turns out the exact same way every time because we cannot control how our oven works, or where the eggs come from, so take the attitude that you will do the very best you can and be successful.

Experiences, good or bad, form our core, our personality, how we react to success, failure and whether we take those learnings to change how we approach life. We can either face them head on or learn what we need to discover and move forward.

I have had many of those situations but the one I would like to share is when I decided, because of a great job offer, to leave everything and everyone to move to London where I still live today. I came to work with a team to launch our publishing company in Europe.

What an amazing adventure and opportunity but I was terrified. I had been to London and parts of Europe on holiday several times but that is nothing like living there. So my journey begins; basically I arrived in the UK and started my new job only to find the company was up for sale, which they knew before they offered me the role. I was upset, and wondering what to do next as I had taken residency in the UK and therefore going back to Canada would be tough. I considered all my options, and did lots of long walks, breathing, spending time alone in nature, talking and spending time with friends and family. When change happens suddenly we panic. My advice is to stop, pause, think about what is good in your life and allow yourself the time and space to grieve.

I decided I could not change what happened but it was my choice how to make this work for me. I learned as much as I could and started looking for another role. I got made redundant, which would have also happened had I stayed in Canada, found a new more senior role and have never looked back. That was 20 years ago and I am still living in a city I adore.

Consider the example below where failure turned into incredible success by changing a point of view. Sometimes all we need to do is stop and review the situation from a different angle. How many have made a cake or pudding that did not work? I have; one time the cake just did not rise enough because the pan was too big, so I split it into layers, added lashings of whipped cream and jam and presto we had a pudding. Not what I had intended but a success. Being able to think on your feet, look at a problem from a different perspective will help change a failure into a learning experience and a potential new product, service or dish. Our attitude makes all the difference. The only thing we can really control is how we react to any given situation – no one can take that from us!

The quote on attitude (over) guides me and helps me deal with obstacles – big, small or just plain annoying – so I hope you find it as useful and uplifting as I do. When I find myself in challenging situations and I struggle to focus on delivering my key goals, I pull out this story.

Attitude

"The longer I live, the more I realise the impact of attitude on life. Attitude, to me, is more important than facts. It is more important than the past, than education, than money, than circumstances, than failures, than successes, than what other people think or say or do. It is more important than appearance, giftedness or skill. It will make or break a company...a church...a home.

The remarkable thing is we have a choice every day regarding the attitude we will embrace for that day. We cannot change our past... we cannot change the fact that people will act in a certain way. We cannot change the inevitable.

The only thing we can do is play on the string we have, and that is, OUR ATTITUDE.

I am convinced that life is 10% what happens to me and 90% how I react to it.

And so it is with you...we are in charge of our ATTITUDES!"

Charles Swindoll

Networking: Who do you know?

Networking is a noun, defined as the act of making contact and exchanging information with other people, groups and institutions to develop mutually beneficial relationships, or to access and share information between computers. Read more at http://www.yourdictionary.com/networking#51ASHtzZRM6FDRWV.99

In Canada I grew up networking, it is part of our DNA. No matter how outgoing you are, networking is still difficult.

There are many different types of networking including face to face and social networks.

Where to start? Having a core of people who you trust and can offer honest advice and guidance is essential. These are the people you turn to when you need help to attack any major challenges. Those you trust, like and respect. This may be only a handful of people.

Ask yourself who do you know that is willing to give you feedback, who offers you a 'sounding board'. This may mean something as simple as chatting with friends and work colleagues and asking for feedback (what they see as your strengths and weaknesses, their perception of what you are great at and love to do). This is hard but important in understanding how others perceive you and how you come across in different situations.

Secondly, try and meet people who are different from you. This is where you can brainstorm and you might come up with a brilliant idea that neither of you would have thought of on your own but together ideas emerge. This network might be much bigger and involve lots of different people from many industries and professions but this is where real change and great ideas happen.

Much has been written about building connections and your network but I believe it is a very personal thing and each person's approach is different. Here are a few things to think about when building your network. Remember we meet people all the time, not just at events.

- Develop a style that works for you

- Be true to yourself and people will respond to you and your personal chemistry

- One way to start is to help other people without expecting anything in return

- Go to events or conferences that you really don't want to attend, as you never know who you might meet

- When at an event or conference set yourself a personal goal of meeting at least five new people

- Through work if you get an invitation to an awards dinner or grand opening because there is a spare ticket available, take it; find out who is attending and decide if there is anyone specifically you want to meet and make it happen

I had a call about an incredible role from a recruitment company asking if I knew of any candidates that would fit the requirements. Three individuals came to mind; I approached each of them, all of whom were looking for a new role. Once I got the OK I suggested they send in their details and then I contacted the recruiter so they could review and follow up accordingly.

There was nothing in this for me, but I know the company and they treat people well, I also realised that these three contacts were looking for work so I put them in touch and hopefully one of them would get the role.

I have found throughout my life, both personal and professionally, whatever you put out there you get back.

And helping others is a good place to start.

Food byte:

I think the definition of a boomerang sums it up perfectly.
Boomerang: 'A returning boomerang is designed to circle back to the thrower' defined by Wikipedia

Do some work and think about what are the top two to three things you want people to remember about you. Maybe you speak three languages, are passionate about people and customer service. Each person is different but this gives those you meet a quick overview of how you can help them or they can help you.

This will also help when it comes time to prepare your CV.

When networking never be negative or disparaging about others, it is unprofessional and it makes people wonder what you might say about them behind their back.

A great suggestion made by Mrs Moneypenny in her book *Careers Advice for Ambitious Women* is to keep a database of those you meet to remember them. She suggests making a note about when you last met, and what you discussed. I think it is a great idea as how many times do we get business cards and then we meet the people again and cannot quite remember how we know them? It is a bit embarrassing so this would put a stop to one challenge. And you never know who you might meet that can change your life.

Create and utilise your work and social network; sites like Facebook and LinkedIn have made this much easier and accessible.

Let's take a moment to consider our virtual networks. For me I use Facebook for my core friends. This is great way of keeping in touch with family and friends who do not live near and I don't get the opportunity to see them enough. I don't use it for my professional network. That doesn't mean you shouldn't but be careful what you put on the site and make sure you use your privacy settings.

LinkedIn is a networking tool that I use more for my professional life. I highly recommend taking a course. I know it helped me uncover all sorts of tools to use when looking for a job. I had an amazing teacher who showed us the power of using this tool correctly and effectively. Make sure your profile is current and keep in touch with your network. Take advantage of the advanced job search function and keep your summary concise using key words that highlight your skills and desired role.

During my last redundancy I decided to work for myself and combine my love of technology and people. I wanted to work in outplacement so I did some research and found out who the UK managing director was in a particular company. I then used LinkedIn to see if I knew anyone who could make an introduction. I was successful and my contact made the introduction, I then met him and I am now working as an associate for the company. The power of the network.

I believe that networking forced upon us does not work. It becomes easy when we meet people who have common interests or are inspired by speakers or courses. When I attend an event my personal goal is to meet at least five new faces, male and female. What is fundamental is managing your network. Also cherish and respect and value your contacts.

Are you maximising the opportunities that exist within these great tools? Creating a network is never easy but think of it as an adventure and a great way to meet new people and learn more about others.

If you have been in the same role and had the same circle of friends for ages, don't hesitate, take your first step in creating that all-important network, ask a friend, join a group that appeals to you even if it is social to ease you in slowly. You will be amazed how quickly this can build.

Do you have a role model? Is there someone who inspires change? It may be someone you work with, or have heard speak or just read about. Katherine Hepburn inspired me as a child because she lived her life to the full. Women like Mrs Moneypenny and Margaret Thatcher are strong, successful and inspirational women.

Look at groups like Meetup which are easy to set up and run depending on what, where and how you want to make it work. A friend of mine wanted to meet new people in her neighbourhood so she set up a networking group and made me the co-founder. We met different people from all walks of life and we've since disbanded the group but some of the people have become great friends.

There are different types of networking groups springing up everywhere; regardless of industry, culture, location, they are at your fingertips. If you ask for help and receive that help it is important that you give back, as the more you help others the more help you receive!

Example: When I wanted to change industry sector and get into technology I met a friend of a friend who happened to be Canadian – she was able to give me great tools to enter the field. And thanks to her I got my first technology role at SAP in the UK.

Who do you look to for support? Who do you believe really understands you (family, friends and/or co-workers or support groups)? Document this as part of your toolkit – think about what you are looking to do – write down names of your contacts next to your ideas to act as a reminder when you are ready.

Access to a computer and the internet remains important as one of your tools whether at home, work or library. Think about what provides you easiest access and plan ahead (if you are at home lots then check out the library or internet café – sometimes a change of scenery is as good as a rest and allows you to focus without the distraction of home).

If buying access then book ahead; if you plan to use a local internet café or the library then check out opening and closing times and cost involved as well as security. Make sure your information is protected.

Research is an essential tool when considering your next step whether that is starting up your own company, getting a promotion, changing industries or facing retirement. Research helps provide key information on companies, roles, education, training, and key skills needed to pursue your dream job.

That means having access to newspapers, internet, company information, background search which is easily found online. Look for company or annual reports, press releases; if the company is privately held it becomes a bit more difficult to get relevant information but search the company and you will be amazed what you can find out.

Also it is amazing what you can uncover by using a search engine like Google. Try looking up yourself and you might be surprised what you find. There are other sources which can be found easily by looking up research tools online. The list is endless.

Cindy Recipe Box

I carry a small notebook with me at all times. I could use my phone but I like putting pen to paper. When I have a great idea or see something that impacts me, I write them down as they come to mind – that way my thoughts are in one place and easy to find and inspirational.

The simple tool and my personal favourite: paper, any type, colour, big or small. I have a huge book of blank paper that I use with different coloured pens so I can write, draw pictures – whatever brings the concepts alive for me. Spending the time putting pen to paper brings things alive for me, do what works for you.

Sometimes a mix of written and online works better – try different approaches until you find what works for you. There is something very special about using colour and images to bring your dreams and goals alive. I think it reminds me of learning to colour when I was a child. Remember how proud we felt when we managed to colour within the lines. So have fun with it and let your imagination run wild.

Another component of your toolkit is a mood board defined by: *http://en.wikipedia.org/wiki/Mood_board*

Use old magazines, newspapers, photos to create a picture of your ideal job or career. This may sound far-fetched and does take dedicated time but once complete you can put it somewhere that you look at every day like the fridge door, leave it in your car, or behind the bathroom door. When you see it daily things start to shift in your mind and your attitude. Think about TV ads or music that you keep hearing; before you know it you remember all the words to the song or the music! Imagine the power this has in helping you get unstuck and moving forward to your next great adventure.

Other suggested tools to add to the all-important kit include music. Some people find listening to specific types of music helps them relax, it may bring images or memories to the front of your mind which in turn may get your creative juices flowing and before you know what has happened you have a view of what to do next. So let your imagination run wild and use what tools work for you!

Food byte:

Creative Visualisation by Shakti Gawain, one of my favourite books, which I still use 20 years later; who knew how important that book became in my life so I recommend it to everyone.

Exercise Time

Complete the following exercise – ideal scene: find a big piece of paper or use your computer and ask yourself the following question:

If I could be, do and have everything I want, what would be my ideal scene?

Break it down into the following areas/examples:

- Work/Career
- Money
- Lifestyle/Possessions
- Relationships
- Creative expression
- Leisure/Travel
- Personal growth
- World/Situation/Environment

Complete a detailed analysis of wants, needs and desires (including financial, emotional, family, promotion, willingness to travel, benefits, training etc.).

Make time for yourself, find a quiet place or corner where you will not be interrupted for at least 30 minutes. This may take more time than you think so don't worry about completing it all at once. Keep coming back to it but the more focused time you can spend, the better. If I could be, do or have anything what would that look like?

Example:
Work/Career

Running a successful business that allows flexibility and variety and is financially and personally rewarding. An opportunity to combine my different skills and experience to help others and focus on the industry and skill set I love.

Keep writing – it may take pages, keep the creative juices flowing!

Step 3a:
Preparation of Ingredients

*"Success depends upon previous preparation,
and without such preparation there is
sure to be failure."*

Confucius

One important key to success is self-confidence. An important key to self-confidence is preparation.

When I was learning to cook my mother taught me that preparation was a key ingredient in cooking. We were taught to check the recipe, find the ingredients and put them in front of us, then methodically read through the recipe and prepare the ingredients as needed. Once you have finished with the ingredients then put them away so you have more space and more importantly you won't add the ingredient twice, and better still there will be less to clean up when you are finished. The same applies to anything we do in life. People spend more time planning a holiday than thinking about their career, which is a bit of a shocker. So let's get your ingredients ready for our pasta dish.

Food byte:

Fill your sink (if like me you don't have a dishwasher) with hot soapy water, when finished with a cutting board or knife you can wash up as you go.

Cindy's Recipe

Finely chop the onion, courgette and garlic making sure all three are similar in size and shape so they cook consistently. No one wants a piece of raw garlic! This applies to anything that you are chopping – vegetables, meat or grinding spices.

Take your pot and add water to it about halfway (depending on how much pasta you intend to use – it expands).

Bring the water to a rolling boil and add a few pinches of salt.

Food byte:

Water boils faster if you put the lid on – then remove the lid when cooking the pasta so it does not boil over.

Once done add the dry pasta (cook to al dente – about 8-10 minutes and please don't forget to taste and check as different types of pasta require different cooking times and fresh pasta cooks very quickly, 1-3 minutes).

Recipe books detail different types of cutting techniques: julienne strips, grated – it's up to you to create the look and taste. Have fun, experiment and let your creative juices flow. Just like life, recipes are made not just to follow but to add your own personal touch and create your masterpiece!

Food byte:

To get the skin off garlic, use the heel of a knife and press down on the garlic clove and the skin should come off easily.

Open the canned tomatoes and drain but reserve the liquid as you might use some or all of it for the sauce (if the pieces are too big you might want to cut them up making sure they are the same size).

Grate the cheese – if you don't have a cheese grater then use a knife or a potato peeler.

Set the table and warm the oven to heat the plates so when serving the food it stays hotter longer. How many times are you in a restaurant and by the time your food arrives it is cold? Good restaurants know how important it is to heat the plates before serving.

Food byte:

When chopping chillies remember to put a bit of olive oil underneath and on your fingertips so the chilli heat stays on the olive oil and not on your fingers.

Food byte:

When I cook I prepare most of this in advance – it makes it quicker and easier to cook when everything is at your fingertips. Not only that but it makes clearing up much easier, that way you can put stuff away as you go which gives you more space especially if like me you have the world's tiniest kitchen. Utilising and maximising space makes a huge difference and getting the dishes washed as you go makes life so much easier.

Step 3b:
Creating Your Picture of Life

"The people you surround yourself with influence your behaviors, so choose friends who have healthy habits."

Dan Buettner

Think about what you would like a camera to capture when you look at your life a few years down the road (a picture of you doing what you love). In his book *The Gift* Shad Helmstetter talks about surrounding yourself with success. He suggests that you imagine a photograph of you surrounded by people who will help you reach your goals and make your dreams come true. Who would you choose to include in your photograph? He goes on to say that many people don't realise how important this is in creating your success.

Remember that what you feed into your brain can mean the critical difference between success and failure. The information on networking and identifying and having your core team. Hopefully many of those individuals are the ones who will support and help you shine and would be in your photograph. What I love about his book is he goes on to state that whether we realise it or not, our computer, our brain is always recording. Critical to understanding this is vital. The unconscious aspect of our brain is taking everything in and storing it as though it's necessary information, even when it is not.

Hopefully by now you have identified your network, made a list of key skills, experiences and have considered your experience (tools) and thought about where you are currently and where you would like to be. It is important to make sure you prioritise those skills and document which of them are transferable to different industries and roles. This works especially well when you are looking to do something different in your career.

Make sure you have everything together; where did you write them down, combine them into one document whether that is a picture mood board, mind map or written long form on paper or on your PC/ iPad, etc.

This step is pivotal – you now have a clear idea of what skills and experience you have, what your perfect role looks like (given you have done the exercise 'If I could' in the previous step).

Remember that exercise I suggested earlier: If I could be, do and have everything I want, what would be my ideal scene?

Exercise Time

Expand the question and break it down in detail if you haven't already: Work/Career, Money and Lifestyle/Possessions – just write what comes easily to you.

Have you listed your core skills? Maybe now you have thought of a few more, you can add them now, this list is a work in progress which may change at any stage depending on you and how well you know yourself.

The work done here will further lay the foundation and just like food preparation is key to making a success of your recipe – saving you time and creating an incredible meal. Include references, letters of recommendation, talk to those individuals and make sure they are happy to do the reference for you, organise them by area and make sure you check their availability.

Food byte:

References should include a mix: professional, personal and business works well.

Example:

- Is it meeting customers and offering excellent customer service? Your client leaves buying more products and feeling great about their purchase.

- Or running a meeting successfully because you are well organised, able to listen to all points of view, keep people to time and on track and accomplish the meeting goals? A real gift!

- Coming up with a creative concept, then presenting the idea to colleagues, getting buy-in, writing the copy and design and turning it into a finished product, design or brochure – maybe it is creating the ultimate Michelin star meal out of few ingredients!

Step 4a:
Bringing the Ingredients Together – Making the Dish

"Food is our common ground, a universal experience!"

James Beard

So all your ingredients are chopped and you are ready to start making your tasty dish. Every experience, whether good or bad, helps make us who we are and this continues as we grow and embrace change. Eleanor Roosevelt said, "Do one thing every day that scares you." Very profound and so true. Stepping out of our comfort zone is necessary so we grow and change - although perhaps not every day. So whether you are new to cooking or an expert, try doing something that gives the dish your stamp. It may be simple like using a different type of cheese or adding more chillies or different herbs, the choice is up to you. Make sure you keep tasting as you go, and don't be afraid to step outside your comfort zone.

I have had many funny stories when it comes to putting the dish together. One of my favourites is a friend who invited a man she liked to dinner. What he didn't know was that she was not a cook but wanted to impress and was willing to step outside her comfort zone and go for it. Her guest was an amazing cook.

Her shopping included a lovely bottle of red wine and her recipe, Cornish game hen (similar to poussin, small guinea fowl in the UK). The bird is stuffed with wild rice and herbs and served with a green salad, he was bringing pudding.

She followed the recipe and prepared her birds. They were in the oven cooking when he arrived. The wine was open, table set and the salad ready when all of a sudden there was a huge explosion. Both of them ran into the kitchen to find Cornish game hen and rice everywhere. She had not realised that wild rice must be soaked first and partially cooked or mixed with white rice as it expands to four times its size. She was mortified but he saw the funny side and they decided that maybe ordering in pizza was the answer.

She fell about laughing and I guess it broke the ice as they went on to marry and she ended up a pretty decent cook. The moral of the story is have fun, take a risk; you never know what will happen. Enjoy each day as time is a precious gift but don't be afraid to step out of your comfort zone.

 ## Cindy's Recipe

Are you ready to start cooking your pasta and sauce?

Now your water is boiling, remove the saucepan lid and add the salt. Add your dried pasta (any type you like) cook for about seven minutes and check to see if it is al dente – slightly hard to the touch.

At the same time start on your pasta sauce and if the pasta is cooked and ready before the sauce, rinse it under cold water so it stops cooking. I do recommend getting the sauce ready before the pasta is cooked as it always tastes best when fresh. Please do not add oil to the water as no one likes slimy pasta. Start bringing the sauce together before you put the pasta in the boiling water so when the pasta is done you can add it to the sauce and keep it hot and fresh.

In a large pan, one that is big enough to hold the sauce and the pasta once cooked, add about one tablespoon of olive oil and cook on a low heat for a few minutes. Olive oil does not do well at very high heat so please keep an eye on it and make sure it is heating up slowly.

Then add the chopped garlic to the warm olive oil and mix together so the garlic flavour infuses with the oil.

Food byte:

Keep the hob on a low heat so you do not burn or singe the garlic; if it burns it will add a bitter taste to your pasta. Also, when preparing the garlic if you cut through and see a green piece in the garlic, remove it as it can make the sauce bitter.

Add the courgette, onion and tomatoes, making sure they have been cut to a similar size and turn up the heat slightly, keep stirring making sure all of them are combined nicely in the oil and garlic, keep moving them around and once cooked turn the heat to a low simmer.

Add a small ladle of water from the pot or some of your leftover tomato juice if you used canned ones, this is a great way to make the sauce go further and keep it healthy. Also the water will have some of the flavour from the pasta water which adds more taste.

Food byte:

If you have Worcestershire sauce why not add a few drops to the sauce and taste, experiment, see what it tastes like as this is about adding another depth of flavour and the same applies if you have a bit of tomato paste or puree.

Add fresh or dried spices, experiment a bit – basil, rosemary, oregano and thyme go well with pasta; fresh herbs like basil are best left to add just before serving.

If you want to make your pasta more filling and go further it is perfect to add leftover chicken, turkey or prawns. This can be added just before you add the pasta, as they are already cooked and just need to be heated through so the additional ingredients are served at the same temperature as the sauce and pasta.

By now the pasta should be cooked, taste a piece to make sure it is cooked the way you like.

Now drain the pasta, but be sure to leave a bit of water in the pot as you might need to add it later.

Taste the sauce and add any spices, now add a little of the pasta to the sauce, coat it with the sauce and once combined add the rest of the pasta and mix through.

The rest is up to you. I add some chopped basil or spinach for colour and a little cheese – bon appetit or enjoy your meal!

Food byte:

Food byte: If the sauce becomes too thick add a little more of the pasta water, this way you save on calories.

Step 4b:
Cooking up YOUR Success

"If you don't like something change it. If you can't change it, change your attitude."

Maya Angelou

Remember we talked about creating the picture of your life today and in the future? How important it is to surround yourself with positive people. Those who support you and help you shine, make you laugh and make the journey a little easier.

In this chapter I want to focus on that concept slightly more.

When we decide to host a dinner party, we plan ahead and there are some fundamental elements which will help us ensure success. We have talked about the picture of you in relative terms in the previous three chapters but I want to focus on this in more detail in this chapter.

Let's bring it alive by using a food example. We have a goal to host a dinner party for six close friends, we decide on the menu: perhaps a starter, main course and dessert. We invite our friends and give them the date and time when the party will take place. What happens next?

Let's break it down. Your goal is the dinner party – goal setting is so important for all of us in life. Why? Those who set goals are far more successful than those who don't. But a goal is no good unless it is written down, and has a specific time frame, just like your dinner party. Each goal could be small or big within a short time frame of a much longer time frame.

How many of you set goals?

To make a goal real, we then consider the goal and break it down. What may stop us from achieving that goal, the obstacles? Once you've done that then an action plan on how to address those obstacles will help start you off in the right direction.

Back to your dinner party goal. Perhaps your obstacle may be finding the right dishes to make and another might be finding the time to complete the dishes, maybe you are trying a dish you have never made and are concerned if it will work. Are you still with me?

Your action plan

1. What dishes to prepare: perhaps you read your cookbooks and pick your favourites, ones you have made before and ask a friend or your partner what they think.

2. When considering the obstacle of time maybe you pick a dish you can prepare in advance and lay the table the night before and buy all your ingredients a few days before and perhaps even do some early prep like chopping some of the components.

3. Finally the wild card, a new dish: try with family or friends before making it for the dinner party to get their feedback and adjust where needed.

I like the analogy of food because it simplifies the process. Many people think they don't have time or know where to start when setting goals. Start with a simple one like the demonstration above.

Maybe committing to exercise or a new food regime or finding your dream job. Don't hesitate, start today.

Food byte:

Set a goal – write it down – set a time frame.

- Write down the obstacles, try to stick to a maximum of five or you might feel overwhelmed

- Then write an action plan to overcome those obstacles and remember to include when and how you will manage to make these a reality

- Set small, medium and large goals

- You might want to create your dream or ideas book for goals

- Break them into different sections like work, spiritual, relationships, financial etc., it is up to you to decide what areas of your life to include in your dream book

Pictures can bring your goal and vision alive so cut out pictures that resemble your desires. Most importantly don't forget to reward yourself when you achieve your goal.

Your goals may change as you achieve some of them, and reward yourself accordingly, write more, it is so important to live your life today as time is such a special commodity. How many of you remember wanting to grow up faster, for a day to pass quickly? My grandmother said to me, "Don't wish your life away, live in the moment and enjoy the bad with the good or how can you appreciate the amazing things that happen? And the older you get, the faster time goes." I miss her guidance and presence every day and I find that as I get older time seems to escape like sand through my hands.

It is precious so enjoy the journey no matter how difficult, sad or happy it is, we can only appreciate success when we experience failure: and know true happiness when we experience loss and sadness. That doesn't mean we don't need to plan for the future, so set those goals, look at them daily and add and change as you continue to live your life. The more you understand what your values and goals are and what the future holds, the better equipped you become to find the job and/or career you desire.

When building your plans and setting your goals, friends, colleagues and family can be an invaluable resource. Once you have a better understanding of where you would like to work and in which role then take a step back and talk to your contacts. Find those that work or know the company and industry really well and can offer you key insights and suggestions for feedback.

Ask if they have contacts within your desired industry or company and would they make an introduction for you. Don't be shy, getting feedback is tough, don't take it personally, rather as a chance to learn without getting defensive.

I remember attending a week-long seminar called 'Investment in Excellence' with my colleagues, which was a real step out of all our comfort zones. We learned how the brain takes in information, how what we say to ourselves creates our destiny. I think it was on day three that we were asked to take a pen and paper and write some positive feedback and room for improvement for four of our colleagues. The feedback was anonymous and the impact huge, there were tears, laughter and discussion and each of us left that room knowing more about how we were perceived by others, and to this day I still have those scraps of paper I read.

Feedback and stepping out of our comfort zone can be tiring and tough for all of us. Create a space where you feel safe to review your actions and feedback.

Exercise Time

Once you have read the material above, take some time and think about purchases or events where the RAS (reticular activating system) has happened to you.

- Write down two key goals that you would like to achieve

- Be sure to add a time frame

- Obstacles in achieving the goal

- An action plan for each obstacle

- And celebrate results

Having done all the previous steps you know what you are looking for, now the question is where do I go to find that perfect job?

The internet is an amazing source of opportunity – there are various job sites where you can submit your CV but using this approach lessens your chance of success. You are one of thousands who may apply for the same role. Recruiters don't know who you are, they review your experience and base their decision on that alone as they have nothing else to compare. Sometimes if you are very lucky and have the perfect skills and experience for the advertised role you might get a phone call. The analogy is like buying a lottery ticket. How often do you expect to win? Remember many roles are never advertised. You need to find a way to stand out from the crowd.

Doing some background work before looking for a role will help you understand what your core skills are, where they fit, which ones are transferable and why. Consider what types of companies appeal to you for various reasons and draw up a list. Prioritise that list, see who you know within those companies using LinkedIn and ask for an introduction or information that may help you move forward and discover the best approach to get through the door.

Volunteering in something that relates to your desired role is very useful. It offers you a chance to try or test it out without leaving your current job or starting a new role only to find it is not at all what you thought it would be. Don't forget when building your CV to include relevant volunteer work like coaching a team (girl guides, boy scouts or a football team) as all of that requires specific skills which may be fundamental in the role you are seeking.

You may have left your current position where you received a great severance package and decided that you want to work for a charity part-time in an area you love. Sometimes multiple options are the new way forward.

If you are in the company and industry you desire but want to change roles then ask if you can shadow the person currently doing the role for a few days. Why? This gives you insights to what the real job is like versus what you think. Very worthwhile, it also shows you are proactive so when new opportunities arise your name may come up before others, enough to get an interview and perhaps the job you want.

This step is about feedback, considering all avenues before you begin the official job hunt. The job hunt is a two-way process: the employer wants a motivated person who fits the needs they identified in their job description. The recruitment process is an expensive one for organisations, it takes time out of key people's day and that is why so many organisations now have an internal talent acquisition initiative. They want to get it right.

If you find the whole process is getting you down, don't get discouraged, re-read the quote by Charles Swindoll on Attitude, take a break and do something you love and then come back to the job hunt. Remember it is like building an extension to your kitchen, it takes planning and putting in the time and energy to get it right. Think back to earlier when I mentioned we spend more time planning our holidays than our careers. We rarely deal with our careers until they are broken and then expect an immediate solution.

The job hunt puts into practice all of the hard work you've completed in the previous steps.

Where to start?

By this stage you should have a clear idea of what your 'recipe of your life' looks like and now is the time for action!

Many find this stage the most difficult but think back to attitude – it is up to you how you approach this task. All of the hard work in the previous steps will make this part of the process a bit easier.

Jobs appear in various ways: online job sites, newspapers, internal websites at your current company, social media (Facebook, LinkedIn), industry magazines (example: *Retail Week* for published roles in the retail sector, *FT* for roles in the finance sector), recruitment companies, head hunters – there are many, do a Google search in your area of interest.

 Cindy Recipe Box

Example: I wanted to share a story about a friend who despite not being a cook decided to make dinner as a thank you for friends. She made lasagne: she made the white sauce (béchamel), it just did not look right but she didn't have time to re-make it so left it as is was, the meat sauce was much easier, and they used pre-cooked pasta which saved time. The dish was ready for the oven. She added one final ingredient, parmesan cheese, to give the top a bit of colour.

Her guests arrived, very excited to be invited to dinner but they were a bit concerned as they had never seen her cook anything! The flat was filled with an aroma of something cooking!

I asked if they wanted any help while they poured drinks so I did the lasagne check. I opened the oven door to find the lasagne rising like freshly baked bread, overflowing into the bottom of the oven – can you imagine? It was funny and we laughed so hard tears were rolling down our cheeks and laughter is good for the soul. They joined in so the disaster was averted.

Turned out she had not checked the label on the cheese and instead of parmesan cheese she added semolina! The lasagne was not her best meal but none of us cared because she had taken a risk and stepped out of her comfort zone to create her near-perfect lasagne!

Exercise Time

Grab a coffee, some paper, laptop, whatever works best for you and draw a table and start filling in what ideal looks like for you when searching for the next role. Refer to the previous information covered in earlier chapters. To make the exercise easier I have given some examples of what you might want to consider.

Ingredients to consider when discovering the right role

Travel time to the office	Ideal 30-60 minutes
Type of company to work for that is ideal (public or private)	Technology company Retailer
Time in terms of hours	Flexible, part-time, full-time
Benefits	Pension, training, holiday, sick time etc.
Salary – what is realistic	Depends on experience, need and industry

Company background	Socially responsible, green, equal opportunity employer
Social	Is it important to have a social component, a real team element, volunteering, support charity?
Work/life balance	Flexibility: taking the children to school, caring for elderly parents

Above are examples to help you start your journey. The list is not exhaustive, some of the areas may be more important to you than others. What I can tell you is that the more time you spend there, the more clarity you get on your 'ideal' – trust me, it works.

Cindy Recipe Box example

Running a successful business that allows flexibility and is financially and personally rewarding. The business would be hands-on but with the ability to grow and extend through various channels.

The job hunt is an interesting journey, by now you should have a pretty clear vision of your strengths and weaknesses by combining all the steps and reviewing them one by one. This includes a summary as described above. You might have also decided that you want to create your own company, which takes you down a different road of research and discovery.

 ## Cindy Recipe Box example

How far do you want to commute? Is the opportunity for advancement important? What about benefits (holidays, pension)? What about the size and type of company: public, government like Transport for London, or private company like a retailer or IT company?

Exercise Time

Take some time to complete the example in my recipe box. Answer the following questions:

1. What type of company would you like to work for and why?

2. Location – what does ideal look like? What is acceptable to you in terms of time spent commuting?

3. Benefits – what type of benefits and salary do you want in your new role?

4. How many hours are you comfortable working? Consider the following: full-time, part-time, shift work, and is flexibility important?

5. Social: is working with a team that works and socialises together important to you?

6. What does ideal look like in terms of your new job?

7. How important is having a work/life balance to you? Today with technology the boundaries become blurred, how can you ensure you achieve that balance?

8. What are you most proud of and why?

9. When managing people how do you handle difficult situations?

10. You are creative when?

11. What satisfies you in work? (working with a great team, variety of work, working under pressure, being challenged etc.).

12. What causes dissatisfaction for you within the work environment?

13. How do you define success? Money, work/life balance?

14. You get stressed at work when what situations arise? How do you deal with those situations?

15. I shine best when?

Step 5a:
Presentation on a Plate

"The way to resumption is to resume."

Salmon Portland Chase

This sounds like a simple step but part of cooking is creating a dish that appeals to our senses. We eat using all five senses even when we don't think about it: the aroma of hot bread, or a steaming plate of pasta as it arrives at the table makes our taste buds salivate and our sense of smell comes alive as our eyes widen in wonder. We cannot wait to taste and see if it lives up to our expectations.

Imagine if someone just threw pasta on a plate, the sauce was everywhere, dripping off the plate, with no visual stimulation at all – would you experience the same reaction if it looked and smelt delicious?

Through a number of different cooking courses, the steps were vital for success but presentation was king. A chef is measured by how the plate appears. These days we are surrounded by cooking programmes and celebrity chefs and we cannot seem to get enough of watching amateurs compete in shows like *The Great British Bake-Off* or *MasterChef*. I love those shows and am passionate about food, it's incredible what you learn just by listening and observing them in action.

I was fortunate enough to do a course at Le Manoir aux Quat'Saisons when I quit my job at Cisco; I only had a week off and decided to spend the money investing in me and my cooking ability. Wow, what an experience – the care and patience spent on making sure the customer's food is perfect. I know why they have the Michelin stars and why people flock to the restaurant. They make their chicken stock using all the wings, these are put in a huge vat and used to give the stock that depth of flavour. Even things like toasting the flour used when making coq au vin, simple yet effective. For them taste is king and making their customers' palates sing is essential. Plating a work of art. I think of chefs as artists, the food looks so good I don't want to take that first bite. How many of you have noticed diners taking photos of their dishes to share with friends? Not sure that happens much in a pub or a fast food restaurant. Whether eating in any type of restaurant we use our senses to taste the food before we take a bite.

This is very important, take time and think about how the dish will look when served, do I use a round or square plate or a bowl? Regardless of the dish, I guarantee it makes a difference. Make sure your plate is clean, no splatters. This also applies when creating your CV, cover letter or application – check for spelling mistakes. Take the time to review and edit to bring out the magic.

I have a personal pet peeve when eating out. How many times does your food come to table and it is cold? In London many diners are on the top floor and kitchen downstairs. Please, I beg you, warm your plates so your food stays hot.

So take your warmed plates, drizzle with a bit of extra virgin olive oil – one teaspoon, not too much, this is more for presentation, when you cooked your pasta you added it to the sauce.

Food byte:

Taste the pasta after it is mixed with your wonderful sauce and adjust seasoning if needed.

Now it is time to take the pasta mixture and place it over the olive oil on your plate. Be creative, put it in a swirl and sprinkle with your choice of grated cheese; what about adding a basil leaf (a wonderful combination with this dish) then perhaps a twist of black pepper and a pinch of salt.

Now your pasta is ready to serve – voilà you've made it – enjoy your hard work!

In this book we have worked though the main dish, but you might want to serve this dish with a side salad or some fresh bread.

Step 5b:
Showing Off Your Credentials – Curriculum Vitae (Résumé)

"Beware of relying solely on a résumé (CV) to hire, skills can be taught.

What cannot be taught is a great 'can do' attitude."

Beth Ramsay

Your CV is crucial to your success. Sometimes it is the first impression a future employer has of you. Think of it as part of your toolkit, we discussed this in Step 2b. Or think about it as a sales tool, a piece of marketing material or brochure that tells your specific story. It tells prospective employers what you have done in the past, where you are currently and what your goals are for the future. Remember, don't give everything away initially, this should be a summary offering the highlights of your career and your significant achievements.

In this step we are going to cover the CV basics, there are so many different ways to write your story. Think about steps one to five that you have worked through in this book. All of that hard work and preparation will hopefully make this step a bit easier.

I suggest taking all the material you created, whether on your computer, bits of paper or pictures and compile all your information then find somewhere you will not be disturbed and review. Once complete start pulling it into a summary and observing your answers, see what jumps out, or where you might need to consider some of the outcomes to help you move on to the writing of your CV.

I assume you have completed the exercises in each of the steps? These lay the foundation for what will become your CV. If you have not completed the questions now might be a great time to stop, go back, review and finish the exercises. Trust me, this helps.

I worked in recruitment for 18 months covering a maternity cover, most of our focus was helping companies find freelancers. During that time I must have reviewed about 2,000 CVs and it was fascinating to see what people included. I remember one individual who presented me with a five-page CV and they were the ripe old age of 25! They had too much personal information. Try and stick to a CV of one or two pages, or three if you are in a more mature phase, depending on your level of experience.

 Cindy Recipe Box example

I did volunteer work for an incredible charity called Beyond Food. Their mission is to help the homeless back into work. They apply for a six-month apprenticeship with Beyond Food and when they complete their six months most will receive an NVQ level 1 & 2 Commis Chef, which puts them on the first rung to becoming a great chef. I ran a group session with individuals who had mixed cooking skills. I was inspired by their creativity: every dish looked completely different, a real variety of flavours and designs, yet all had used exactly the same ingredients. It is that 'personality' that makes the difference. Make sure your CV shines and reflects your key differentiators. What makes you stand out?

CVs come in different shapes and sizes. Every CV must include some specific information so that it makes it easy for the recruiter or employer to understand your past, present and future plans. Your future can be summarised by writing a professional objective. Including this is a personal choice. I use one as it helps the recruiter or employer understand what you want to do next. This may change depending on the role.

My CV changes constantly and I have about six different versions because I adjust each one depending on the role or contract I am interested in winning.

As an example, my background is in sales, marketing, business development, stakeholder analysis and alliances so I try and sharpen my CV to highlight the different areas desired by my future employer.

I believe that a CV should include the following:

Basic information or a heading

This includes your name, address, contact details, some people include a photo and some a video clip, that is up to you.

Company information

If the company you work for is not a known brand then write a brief description of what that company does. One or two lines should be enough. When I worked for HP someone thought I meant HP sauce! I thought the brand was everywhere but this proved my point so capturing the essentials of the company will help potential employers. This is especially relevant when you want to move outside your industry sector.

Professional objective and summary

This is optional and is more relevant for certain types of backgrounds. This can also be called 'my next role' - just a few lines to show the reader your goal or what you want to do next for work. If it is not there readers will assume you want to continue and do a similar job to your current role. This is your story, so make it real, be able to support your statements and remember to keep it short and focused, include your personal summary or profile.

This step is fundamental to success and one of the most difficult because it is awkward for most of us to sing our own praises. Shine in your CV, it gives your potential employer a quick insight to your goals, ambitions and successes and should be tailored depending on who you are sending your CV to in terms of company and industry.

Some include a summary statement, this can be very relevant if you have specific skills which may be technical.

Work or employment history

Include a brief description of what your company does, this will help your potential employer understand and reference facts. Be sure to include a list of your main responsibilities within that specific role, be as brief as possible but use action words to highlight key areas.

Once that is done, don't forget a list of your achievements. For your current job no more than six and think about the performance measurement that is relevant for your specific industry or profession.

List your role, for example: Marketing Director, Head of Business Development, Financial Controller, Operations Manager or Director and the details of start date to finish. What were your key responsibilities and key activities? Please try to use action words and keep this precise and short.

I carry a small notebook with me and when I have a few moments I jot ideas down. I think about my job description, analyse it step-by-step then detail things that highlight my accomplishments including the objective and outcomes. It is up to you to make yourself shine. The hardest thing for many of us is talking about our achievements.

This is an excellent way to use your commute. Before you know it the journey is complete and you made progress in documenting key facts and figures. Take the concepts and bring them alive with examples of success and where possible make sure those successes are quantifiable.

 Cindy Recipe Box

If you are a professional such as an accountant, lawyer, trader, teacher, highlight your professional designations (e.g. Institute of Chartered Accountants) and whether you are an active member or not. This is important, especially if you get involved, as not only will you meet people with similar experiences you also might find your next role. It demonstrates initiative.

Advertising or Marketing: include a portfolio and professional organisations you belong to or courses completed (e.g. CIM, Institute of Direct Marketing).

There are numerous resources available and services to help you pull the right CV together for your specific skills (visit your local library or job centre and go online, the resources and help available is incredible).

Technical CTO, IT Director: list professional designations but also some of the key projects that were successful and some cutting edge new technologies. Try to demonstrate in two lines or less a few core achievements. Tailor your CV to the job you are applying for – I know this take ages and is a real pain but it works and shows you have read and understand the job description and made the effort to make the CV as impactful as possible.

If in your desired role a requirement is to do public speaking then include relevant experiences like doing guest lectures to 300 students, workshop facilitator where you had 25 attendees, and a rating of 4 out of 5.

Working in virtual teams is a key skill when working for technology companies. As a contributor, given the depth and breadth of working from home, using video and web conferencing, reaching across country borders, means you must demonstrate where this has been done before; make it real, this is essential. The more you quantify with examples, the more you will bring your experience and background alive for the reader. Recruiters or HR directors may receive hundreds of potential candidates' CVs. Think about how to make yours stand out, how can you bring it alive and make them want to interview you?

Cindy's example

Identified new industry experts willing to make introductions into senior decision makers resulting in five new contacts and potential pipeline of £5 million.

Food byte:

If you have worked for the past 10 years, your education is not (in most cases) as important as where you have demonstrated how that education has been used in one of your roles. It is about the application and experience, not your education. Personal details are not as relevant so keep it simple.

One piece of advice is once your CV is complete, send it to someone who knows you well and has done similar roles and ask for feedback. Incorporate their suggestions and finally get someone to write it for you professionally if English is not your first language or you are not the best writer.

Food byte:

Responsible for developing new business, from zero sales to 10 million within one year... write down briefing your key areas followed by an outcome – whether qualitative or quantitative they both show that you are capable of delivering.

I see many people who have worked for one organisation for many years. It is important to demonstrate within your CV the different roles and responsibilities held within your last company. Highlight the role then state what part of the company, this is important especially for big corporate organisations. What you want to communicate to future employers is your ability to grow with your current company, to show even though your employment has been with one organisation you moved around, and as your expertise and experience grew you were able to get promoted into areas perhaps outside your comfort zone. A willingness to take on new assignments and projects and grow demonstrates your flexibility and interest to potential employers.

What happens if you have done freelance work or were self-employed? How do you position and explain those assignments within your CV?

I had this dilemma when I was updating my CV. I have worked freelance and also on PAYE. I had a heading that listed Interim, with a heading either Consultant or Marketing Director. This gives the impression of more stable employment but also shows the reader what you actually did within those interim or freelance roles.

Demonstrate ability and achievements. It takes a very confident, self-starter and well organised person to work freelance or as an interim. You must be able to walk into the role, meet the key people, understand the company's key deliverables and be clear on what is expected of you. This is not an easy thing to do. Some people decide to give this a go when they have been in senior positions but are not clear on their next steps. This allows you to work in a different role or sector. It is not for everyone but it can be incredibly rewarding, scary and wonderful.

If you want to pursue this avenue please do your research and talk to friends or colleagues who have experience working interim. There are also financial implications. You may be paid as a contractor for a specific time frame, covering a maternity leave, or filling a skills gap and they will pay you a specific amount of money via PAYE, including bank holidays and holiday pay. The other option is setting yourself up as a limited company on a daily rate or for a specific project rate (example: the company required a marketing strategy for a new product) with the company determining the time, resource and budget required. This is essential so you get what is best for you and the company.

When it comes to actually writing your CV there are different formats.

Chronological

This is when you take your current job and work backwards. This works when you have had continual job growth and promotion but not so helpful when you want to change careers.

Functional CV

This is much more about stressing your qualifications. This is great when you want to show your skills because you are looking at a different industry. You want to show that the skills and qualifications are transferable.

Cindy Recipe Box

When working in publishing I was impressed by the direct marketing skills of my colleagues. Publishers work to tight budgets and time frames. Many don't use agencies so as a marketer you must be open to doing the writing, budgeting, time management and concepts and deliver them perfectly. So when I did a freelance role in recruitment many of my telecommunications clients needed strong direct marketers but they were in short supply. I suggested they look at candidates on my books from the publishing world as I knew they would deliver the goods on time. Technology companies were very open to giving it a go, this was for a three-month freelance role and the outcome was always positive.

Remember the quote earlier: You can learn the industry but it is your transferable skills and positive attitude that makes the difference.

I highly recommend looking online to see samples of different CVs. This will help you determine what works best for your specific experience and expertise.

Step 6a:
Relax, Your Meal is Complete. What's Next?

"You learn a lot about someone when you share a meal together."

Anthony Bourdain

I find entertaining fun, hard work, a test in preparation, creativity and a great way to show your friends and family you care. Good friends are to be treasured and nurtured and food is my way of reaching out and bringing these amazing friends together.

After everyone has eaten, it is time to clear up. Hopefully, because I tend to clean as I go given I have a small kitchen, and I reuse some of the plates and without a dishwasher, it makes life much easier.

I love listening to my guests and getting their feedback, what they loved, but mainly the easy conversation and laughter is what makes my night. Watching them as they taste the food and the expression, whether good or bad it doesn't matter, it always makes me smile. As we near the end of my story it reminds me of many times after a dinner party or a gathering of friends about what else I would love to try next time. I relax by reading food magazines and watching food shows, it is wonderful all the little nuggets of information you can gather.

If you are still reading then hopefully food has unlocked some ideas, offered hope and inspiration. One of my favourite things about cooking for others is seeing them dig in, enjoying every bite. Sometimes I look up and see people so intent on enjoying their meal there is complete silence until one pauses to take a sip of their drink – how wonderful to share the gift of food with friends and family. Now the fun begins, clearing the dishes and tidying up the kitchen. "A good cook always cleans up their mess," is what I remember hearing from my mum as a child, she used to say that continually and I guess it has stayed with me ever since. I grew up in a family of eight where money was tight and food precious. Nothing was wasted and we ate what was put in front of us, at least most of the time.

My mother loved having a big family and all of us ate together for dinner. She had this incredible way of making food go further. For instance, she would take mince and add porridge oats making it more nutritious and filling. It wasn't until I moved out that I realised most people did not add oats to their burgers. Despite no second helpings she never turned away unexpected guests. She would add another potato to the pot or a bit more pasta and sure enough no one ever left hungry. All of our puddings were home-made and one of my personal favourites was oatmeal cookies. Many great debates and discussions were had at the dinner table especially on a Sunday when our grandparents joined us. As a teenager I disliked being forced to have dinner with everyone, yet what do you think I missed the most when I moved away?

Sometimes it was difficult to be heard so I learned to speak up, ask questions and not be shy. That has helped me to this day when being interviewed or interviewing either for a job or when I was in business selling.

When the dishes are done and our guests have left, we review the evening, the conversations, the food and the wine and wonder about our next party. Living in London allows me to explore amazing market stalls and areas with every possible ingredient available; for a girl growing up on the prairies this was not the case. Food was grown in our garden in the summer and come autumn it was picked, frozen, preserved for the long winter months ahead. Even now when I am back in Winnipeg at Christmas many of the ingredients we take for granted are hard to find and quite costly.

Street food is having a huge resurgence in the UK as more and more people want to share their culture and food. Many people have set up their own food vans, tired of expensive restaurants where getting good, tasty, consistent food is difficult. Michelin-starred restaurants while delightful are only affordable a few times a year.

Growing up in Canada we lived among so many cultures that we tried different types of cuisine while still very young: French, Chinese, Thai, German, Italian, Russian, Japanese and Ukrainian – incredible. I believe this inspired my love of food. I also think that is what makes Canadians great travellers, eager to experience and try different cultures and cuisines.

I get asked many times what my favourite Canadian dish would be. What food in Canada stands out? That is tough given we are a cultural mosaic, a country formed by so many others. Maple syrup, back bacon, venison and bison might represent a few. For me my memories include eating cabbage rolls or pierogi at my Ukrainian friend's house after school; pasta, Hungarian goulash, Chinese, Italian or Portuguese custard tarts with different friends.

Every August bank holiday in Winnipeg they host a huge festival called Folklorama, which started in 1970 and now continues for two weeks in August. This is where different groups host music, provide food to appreciate and respect cultural differences and motivate people to take pride in their own cultural heritage. Everyone gets a passport and is encouraged to get as many stamps as possible. As children we looked forward to participating and attending. What a wonderful way to introduce generations to food and respect different cultures.

This section highlights a bit of planning, appreciating food and different cultures and the importance of understanding each other and how important that family connection is, not only with relatives but with those we gather into our life, our friends and colleagues, sometimes closer to us than blood relatives.

By now you have your CV pretty much ready and you have networked with friends, family and colleagues. You have a clear goal on what you want to do next, and have a plan in place to turn your goal into a reality, one step at a time. Remember, just like preparing a dinner party and cleaning up afterwards, preparation is the key to success.

Now you are at the interview stage, and as Bill Gates said, "We all need people to give us feedback. That's how we improve."

Step 6b:
Business Side, the Job Interview

"The future belongs to those who believe in the beauty of their dreams."

Eleanor Roosevelt

Expect the unexpected for this is key to getting the role of your dreams! Make an impression, be prepared and understand the interview process.

The interview process is perhaps the most important part of the whole process. If you are like most people you will go through several interviews, offers and negotiation before getting the job you want.

The interview is a two-way process, contrary to what some people believe the process should never be passive. The interviewer wants to find out if you are the right fit for the role not just in terms of experience and credentials but culture as well. It is very important to make sure you are prepared ahead of the interview. For you it is equally important that they are the right fit for you based on all the work you have done in the previous steps. What kind of organisation is the best or right fit for you?

 Cindy Recipe Box hint

If you have not had many interviews you might need or want to practice – I have a friend who used to get her dad to act as the interviewer and it helped her get prepared. His phrase was 'PMA = Positive Mental Attitude'.

I was working for a hardware company as a freelancer and decided it was time to make a move. I started to attract opportunities (I know it sounds funny but whatever you put out in this world the mind is a powerful force in helping you make it happen). I met a former colleague and mentioned I was looking to change, she immediately told me about a company that was looking for someone with my skillset. I sent her my CV and within 24 hours I had three calls from the company for three different opportunities. Nine interviews and a few months later I was offered and accepted a role I did for the next five years. It took that long because even though they wanted me for the role they had to operate within specific budgets and time frames. Many of those interviews were virtual, covering different business units and countries. One of the interviews was with our Swedish manager, when he found out I was Canadian and from Winnipeg the interview took a different turn to ice hockey. His favourite team was the Winnipeg Jets – you never know what questions will come up so be prepared.

> "Believe in yourself and all that you are.
>
> Know that there is something inside you that is greater than any obstacle."
>
> **Zig Ziglar**

The key to success is preparation

There are many components to think about when getting ready for your interview.

1. If possible find out the name of your interviewer, what their role is and then do your homework. Depending on the person and the role, check to see if they have a LinkedIn profile. This will give you a top line view of their background and experience and a photograph. Google contains an incredible amount of information and can be a valuable asset depending on their profile and role.

2. Research the company and the industry sector. The more homework you do on finding out about the company by reading their annual reports or finding information using search engines for news on the organisation, the better. Being able to talk about the specific sector, whether it is in financial services, retail, pharma, know the challenges, opportunities and threats for that specific area. If you have friends, family or colleagues who know the industry or company ask them for some information. Check LinkedIn and find out if you know anyone who knows your interviewer, then reach out to them for information. This can be the icing on the cake!

3. Prepare a list of questions you think they may ask along with your desired response; this is a two-way process as I mentioned above so all the ingredients need to be added in a methodical manner.

4. Get your story right – what is your current situation? If you were made redundant be ready to talk about why without bitterness or anger, present this as a new opportunity. Be sure you have your credentials and examples ready in a concise format. Your CV opens the door, as we talked about earlier, but always keep something back – a story or anecdote. Think back to what are the core skills they are looking for in this new role and match them to your experience. For example, one key skill is being decisive. Demonstrate a situation and the outcome. I worked in recruitment filling in for a maternity cover running a team of two. We specialised in placing freelancers in marketing roles across technology, publishing and government. I worked

with a brilliant team in a very positive environment. We placed many individuals and I read hundreds of CVs. Many of our candidates were placed in industries they had not worked in before because they had transferable skills and we highlighted the skills with the hiring manager. Most of them got the role because they were prepared, had stories to tell and had a great positive attitude. Very important especially in the freelance world when you are expected to step into a role and run with it, with little or no help from others.

5. Achievements – for each of your previous roles be prepared to talk about outcomes you are most proud of and why. The more you can show positive impact on the company's bottom line, ROI, maximising budget, resource, the better. I see lots of CVs where achievements are mentioned but there is no quantifiable outcome. Always think about the SO WHAT! Think about a situation and how you handled it and don't forget to talk about the results.

6. Be punctual and dress appropriately. Sometimes being late happens especially living in a large city like London so leave earlier, or even better I have been known to check out where I am going the day before so I don't get lost. I always arrive early, prepared with a book and find a café to chill out. Please be sure to dress for the occasion. That may vary depending on the role but always look tidy and well groomed. I had a few candidates in recruitment who did not get the job because they wore jeans to an interview – OK if you are going to see a builder as long as the jeans are clean and you

have a crisp white shirt and jacket. Some women wore jumpers or blouses too low cut or a skirt too short which made both them and the interviewer uncomfortable. It is common sense and if in doubt ask a friend you trust to help recommend an outfit to fit the interview.

7. When being interviewed it is OK to stop, take a breath, pause and answer when YOU are ready. Pauses are good and work well to throw the person off course. Sometimes interviewers have never done this before. They may be scared and if work has been really busy they may not have had enough time to prepare, so make it easy for them. You will get them on your side easily. Regardless of the techniques or experience the role requires, use your accomplishments, stories which relate to a situation, the obstacles you faced, how you dealt with those challenges and the outcome or results. These illustrate your core competencies and behaviour better than anything so prepare at least two examples for each of your roles focusing on your latest job.

8. Ask for feedback when you have answered and asked questions. For instance, do they believe I have the right skills and abilities for the role? And would they consider me a good fit for the organisation? Don't be afraid to ask for feedback, it will help you understand what you might need to do differently at your next interview. It might also identify an area that you can improve. You might get a wonderful surprise!

9. Don't forget to send a thank you email or letter just to let them know you appreciated their time. If the role is a real possibility tell them how much you look forward to working for them. Ask if they need further information or clarification on any points raised in the interview.

10. You may need to go through several interviews before you get your desired role. Each interview is great practice where you learn, observe and fine-tune your skills. Be a sponge and absorb as much as possible and ask for feedback. If you are unsure about a question ask for clarification. Also taking your time to think through your response is good. Taking a breath and a pause is good for both of you and it does help you relax.

11. There are usually difficult or sensitive questions – just like making a soufflé some recipes are harder than others. Questions around why did you leave your last employer? What did you like about your job and what did you dislike? Tell us about a situation where you were criticised and your reaction. What would you say are your weaknesses? What is your current salary expectation? The more time you take to prepare for each and every interview the more positive the outcome will be. Taking all feedback on board as mentioned above can help with other interviews. Be sure to have your stories with results ready.

As Steve Jobs said, *"The only way to do great work is to love what you do. If you haven't found it yet, keep looking. Don't settle."*

Food byte:

If you are feeling nervous because of your interview or a specific question, silently count to ten, breathe, giving you time to collect your thoughts and think about what answer to give your interviewer.

"What lies behind us and what lies before us are tiny matters compared to what lies within us."

Ralph Waldo Emerson

 Cindy Recipe Box - interview

Scenario

You are offered an interview at a bank in the City, you will be seen by three people in different roles within the bank but are not clear on what they do or much about the company.

Situation for you: What should you do to prepare?

1. Write down the situation, obstacles and an action plan and include the company name, now look on the web for information, try and find their annual report and highlight key facts and newsworthy items that would impact the job you are applying for and become familiar with the highlights.

2. Are any of the people interviewing you mentioned in the report, because if they are that will give insight into their roles and responsibilities and an understanding of their influence.

3. Google the interviewers – this can be an amazing source of information especially if they are senior people.

4. Prepare at least five questions based on your findings you think they will ask, given your CV and achievements; there are three interviewers so prepare some of each.

5. Prepare your answers – tell a story which shows a situation, an overview of the challenges you faced along with how you dealt with the situation and the outcome.

6. Write three questions that you would like to ask (I always have an extra two as the more 50/50 you can make the dialogue, the better the interview.

7. Know where the company is located, determine how long it takes to get there and add 30 minutes; it is always better to be early than late.

After the interview

Congratulations, you finished your interviews and the great news is you have been offered a job.

Negotiation

This is a vital step in making sure you get the package you want that fits your needs. Think back to earlier steps, the area around what ideal looks like to you. Go back and read what you wrote down then compare to the package on offer.

It never hurts to take a few days to review and go back to your potential employer with questions. Maybe you would like a bit more money but they have no more budget. Think outside the box.

When I moved to the UK a friend offered me great help with my negotiation. They could not offer me more salary but what I was able to negotiate was a car allowance, six months where they contributed to my rent and one extra month's money in my bank account as well as paying for a hotel for an additional month while I got settled. This made up a huge shortfall in the initial offering and shows you can ask for what you want, always within reason, making sure both you and the employer get what they want. Sometimes you must be willing to back down or walk away. The choice is up to you.

This is not always easy to do and asking someone you respect who has the right experience to review the offer is a brilliant way to prepare for negotiations. Just like the interview, the more prepared you are, the better. That person might also offer insights and solutions that never occurred to you which is gold dust and could change the outcome.

Communicate your needs early so you can build your start date around expectations. There have been times when a role was offered to me and they wanted me to start immediately. Most of us, unless we are freelance or contractors, have notice which our employers may want us to work out or go on gardening leave. Make sure you are aware of what those terms are and be prepared to negotiate if needed. Sometimes you need to delay the start date but make sure when applying and interviewing you understand your new employer's timescales and needs. I have also seen people panic because they had a trip booked and are afraid they won't be able to take the scheduled holiday. When you accept the role be sure to let them know you have a holiday booked and paid for and build it into your terms of employment.

One role I accepted in November and told them I had a trip booked to Canada, they were fine with that but we agreed it would not be paid as I had not accumulated any holidays yet, but within a week of starting I had a death in the family and they sent me home early and paid for the extra days off. I was blown away by their compassion and generosity.

Exercise Time

Take a break, get comfortable! Read through each of the questions below and write down your answers. Some of these were asked in an earlier exercise but I want to make sure you are as prepared as possible so your negotiation goes well.

1. What is your current salary?

2. What are your salary expectations for your next role?

3. How much holiday time are you expecting?

4. Do you have a holiday already planned? Make sure you let them know upfront.

5. Is having a flexible benefit plan important to you?

6. Is paying London Weighting needed for you to take the job?

7. How many hours do you want to work?

8. Is having a flexible work schedule important in your decision? This means you are required to be in the office some days but allowed to work flexitime (in terms of hours) and able to work at home one day a week.

9. How much do you expect them to contribute to a pension plan?

10. Is training and development important to you?

11. How important is getting promoted?

12. Do they offer on-boarding? This helps ease your transition and allows you to meet your colleagues and stakeholders.

13. How important is a private healthcare plan or gym membership?

14. Are flexible benefits important?

Negotiation continued

By taking the time to work out what is important in terms of work, salary, daily rate, benefits (detail which ones), pension, flexible working and/ or training will help make your transition easier. Is flexibility something you want? Whether office based or working from home a few days a week, making that transition to a new role can be daunting and a bit scary. Don't worry, there are some steps to take to help you prepare.

Having changed roles several times I still find day one challenging, everything and everyone is new. Finding out how to get to the new office, getting everything you require to do your role. That fear in the pit of your stomach, sweating, nervous but on the outside trying to appear calm, cool and collected. I have some funny stories. Once I was so nervous I caught my shoe on the carpet and almost went flying like a bird, luckily there was a chair handy which I grabbed then quickly checked to make sure no one else had spotted my near miss.

I now take several deep breaths before I walk into the new office and meet the team or HR and try to calm myself down; I can still feel my hands shake and my stomach knot but that is part of the adventure. Someone said to me if we don't push ourselves outside our comfort zone every day we are not living life to the full.

The more prepared you are, the better. As you read earlier, knowing the location and who you are meeting first helps calm our nerves.

Most companies have an on-boarding process where they set up meetings so you can meet your key stakeholders and settle into the role. You can always ask about this in the negotiation phase. Also along with the on-boarding they should provide the equipment and passwords needed.

If you are working as a contractor, freelance or interim this may not be the case. You will be expected to get up to speed quickly without much help.

When you discuss the role and are negotiating find out as much information as possible including:

- Who are the key stakeholders?

- What are their roles and what are they measured on? See if you can find them on LinkedIn, ask if any of your contacts know them and if they can offer advice on how they work, personally, and ask for advice.

- Do your research before accepting a role. With freelance, agree method of invoice and payment upfront.

- Before starting your first job don't forget to think ahead, what you felt your strengths and weaknesses were in previous roles. Are there steps you can take to address those now so you are ready to deal with them differently if they come up again?

Transitioning to a new company, maybe industry and a new role is a great experience but it can be scary. Depending on how long you were with your last employer everything will seem strange and new. We all have a tendency to compare our last environment with our current one.

I for one am guilty of starting a new role coming in full of new and exciting ideas ready to jump and make the assumption that my colleagues are with me. I found out painfully that approach does not work. I came into my new role at a software company full of what I thought were fantastic ideas that had worked well at a previous role within retail. I noticed within five minutes I lost their attention so I quickly changed the topic to get them back on board. That was the last time I voiced an opinion. What I discovered was that this company was not open to ideas that came from another organisation. Only when I approached things in a consultative manner did I get buy-in.

My advice is to ask questions, listen, learn and observe before you assume that how things were done in your previous company is far better than at your new one. Nothing annoys your colleagues more than saying 'at X we did this'. There probably are better and more efficient ways to perform certain tasks but better to wait until you have been there a while to make your points as subtly as possible.

Present your ideas as: 'What about?' or 'Have you thought about this, have you heard?' etc. Get their buy-in by being inclusive and offering them the chance to voice their ideas and let them take you through from start to finish. The results are incredible.

Congratulations, you have successfully managed to negotiate your terms, you have a start date and understand your roles and responsibilities. How exciting, now the real journey begins!

Summary

"When you are inspired by some great purpose, some extraordinary project, all your thoughts break their bounds. Your mind transcends limitations, your consciousness expands in every direction and you find yourself in a new, great and wonderful world.

Dormant forces, faculties and talents become alive, and you discover yourself to be a greater person by far than you ever dreamed yourself to be."

Patanjali

I hope this book has encouraged you to take that first step. I know how difficult that first step can be. It is easier to stay where we are regardless of whether we are happy because it is a known, a given – that makes us feel comfortable and change is scary. It becomes part of our comfort zone, a daily habit and breaking that habit to move into unknown territory requires preparation, planning and courage.

Fundamental to my success was being lucky enough to work with a fabulous network of friends, family and colleagues who were there to support me every step of the way. Without friends, colleagues and contacts my journey would tell a very different story.

When I got that next role I made sure to say thanks, and help others when they needed advice, guidance or just a friendly ear. The adage says what we put out there we get back. Karma.

So how has the cooking and job hunt been? I hope you have found the book useful, fun, interesting and now feel much better prepared to start your new adventure. Or by incorporating some of the suggestions in the book you have found either a new role that you love or started on a new positive adventure.

How did you find the cooking lesson – did it inspire and encourage you? Have you uncovered your desire to find a new role, connect with friends, family and colleagues and created a new love affair with food?

This book is a culmination of my life adventures from working in Canada and Europe, all the different roles, whether difficult or fabulous, have taught me that the biggest string I have is my attitude to life and how I respond to any situation.

I would love to hear your story, your hints and tips, whether it be around creating a new recipe, or a different way to create your personal CV story or how you approach the job search, interview or new ingredient.

Suggested Further Reading/ Definitions

Another component of your toolkit is a mood board defined by:

http://en.wikipedia.org/wiki/Mood_board – use old magazines, newspapers, photos to create a picture of your ideal job or career.

Creative Visualization by **Shakti Gawain** – my favourite book is one found here which I still read 20 years after making this purchase. Who knew how important that book became in my life so I recommend it to everyone, link here:

http://www.shaktigawain.com/products/books/creative-visualization

The Gift by **Shad Helmstetter**

http://www.amazon.co.uk/s/?ie=UTF8&keywords=the +gift+shad+helmstetter&tag=googhdr21&index=stripbo oks&hvadid=4130873023&hvpos=1t1&hvexid=&hvnetw =g&hvrand=857180401871754249&hvpone=&hvptwo= &hvqmt=b&ref=pd_sl_4l80sz3ao8_b

What Color is Your Parachute? by **Richard N Bolles**
– inspirational and one I have used over the years. It can be found on Amazon.

Top 10 steps to a successful CV:

http://www.totaljobs.com/careers-advice/cvs-and-applications/successful-cv

What to Say When You Talk to Your Self by Shad Helmstetter

http://www.amazon.co.uk/s/?ie=UTF8&keywords=what+to+say+talk+yourself&tag=googhydr21&index=stripbooks&hvadid=7974374793&hvpos=1t1&hvexid=&hvnetw=g&hvrand=4757707691332063592&hvpone=&hvptwo=&hvqmt=b&ref=pd_sl_4vbl2s1xiv_b

The Road Less Travelled by Scott Peck

http://www.amazon.co.uk/Road-Less-Travelled-Arrow-New-Age/dp/0099727404

Rebooting Work by Maynard Webb and Carlyle

http://www.amazon.co.uk/Rebooting-Work-Transform-How-Entrepreneurship/dp/1118226151

Appendix: Goal Setting

Goal setting is a key component of achieving your dream desire:

- A goal is not a goal unless it is written down, with a timeline in the next column

- Write the goal in the present tense

  Example: my goal is to have a new job within six months

- Once written down with a timeline (suggest starting slowly) – be realistic

- Now think about each obstacle that may stop you from achieving your goal – write them down

- Beside each obstacle write an action plan with time frames

- Once complete be sure to revisit your written goals weekly

- Once you reach a goal please reward yourself

- Remember people who set goals and review them consistently achieve 90% more in realising their dreams and true path

Cindy's Recipe:
Spaghetti with Courgette

Ingredients

- One or two handfuls of pasta

- 1 small courgette chopped

- 1 clove of garlic finely minced

- 50 grams of grated parmesan cheese

- 2 green onions finely diced (if you don't have a green onion replace with one shallot or small white onion)

- 1 can of chopped tomatoes

- Handful of either fresh or frozen basil (hint in the book: we only have frozen basil. Tip: if you have fresh herbs left over just throw them in the freezer and use frozen)

- 1 tablespoon olive oil

Method

- Chop all the ingredients so they are similar sizes (that way they cook uniformly)

- Put cold water in a good size saucepan and bring to a boil with the lid on

- Heat up your frying pan, add about 1 tablespoon of olive oil – make sure the pan is large enough to hold the sauce and pasta

- Heat the frying pan slowly – now add the garlic (make sure the pan is not too hot or the garlic will burn and taste bitter)

- Check if the water is boiling, remove the lid, add about 1 teaspoon of salt which will keep the water boiling and add flavour to the pasta

- Add the pasta – move it around so it does not stick together (dry pasta can take anywhere from 7-9 minutes so check it and be sure to taste, it should still be firm to the touch)

- Now add the green onion and courgette (that way the courgette will take on the flavour of the garlic, onion and oil)

- Stir for a few minutes then add the can of tomatoes

- At this point you might want to add a ladle full of the pasta water

- What I sometimes do, if you have it on hand is add a few dashes of Worcestershire sauce and/or tomato puree

- Keep stirring the sauce on a low heat and taste – you might need to add salt and pepper; if I have leftover goat's cheese I whisk a bit into the sauce

- Check the pasta – once done, drain and add to the sauce

- Voilà – taste and season – now add the cheese

- Drizzle your bowl or plate with a teaspoon of extra virgin olive oil

- Now dress your plate with the pasta and sauce

Enjoy!

About the Author

Hailing from Canada, Cindy has lived in the UK for over 20 years. During her working life, she has changed industries several times, moving from retail to criminal justice, followed by publishing, recruitment, technology, marketing and, more recently, career consulting. Cindy also has a lot of experience with redundancy, having lost her job four times in the span of 20 years. On other occasions, it was Cindy who decided to change roles, knowing that she could develop herself and her skills further if she took up another opportunity. Currently, Cindy is an Associate Consultant with Lee Hecht and Harris, one of the largest companies in talent acquisition and career development in the UK. Until recently she was also also Chief Marketing Officer for Vizolution, a technology startup.

Cindy is also a professional speaker, facilitator and cook. Her speaking engagements include the 1994 Commonwealth Games in Victoria, Canada and guest lecturing on marketing and sales at many Canadian and UK universities. While at Cisco Systems, she presented to big retail brands across Europe on retail, technology and the future, and more recently, while at SAS UK, spoke on radio about the importance of analytics and the customer journey.

She loves sales, marketing, uncovering new opportunities, exploring ideas and helping people reach their potential and find their true vocation. In addition, Cindy is passionate about food and cooking, the fruits of which bring great joy to her friends and family whenever they have the opportunity!

The ability and courage that Cindy has to pick herself up when a job disappears or to leave a good position for something that inspires her more are the ingredients of her latest business venture: Cooking up Success. While her career path has involved significant challenges, lots of tears and laughter and a great deal of learning, Cindy is now in a place that makes her happier than she could have imagined. She is now her own boss, working with the three pillars that give her life true meaning: people, food and technology.

She is passionate about helping people find their preferred working role and through her new venture plans to support people in finding their own courage to pursue their true vocation in life and to show them through food, cooking and technology that they already have most if not all of the skills and knowledge to do so. She knows that by sharing her experiences and stories she can help others who are facing redundancy, retirement or other changes to learn from the past, to believe in themselves, and to discover their true potential. They might just learn some new cooking tips along the way as well!